Howard Kasschau

PIANO COURSE

Step-by-Step to Mastery of the Piano

PRIVATE or CLASS INSTRUCTION

Illustrated by Josine Ianco Kline

ED. 2348

G. SCHIRMER, Inc.

DISTRIBUTED BY

HAL•LEONARD®
CORPORATION
7777 W. BLUEMOUND RD. P.O. BOX 13819 MILWAUKEE, WI 53213

CONTENTS

TO THE TEACHER

Book Two of the *Howard Kasschau Piano Course* is designed to develop an understanding and means of expression in music. Music expresses feelings, thoughts, and the experiences of daily events, using tones rather than words to do so. Through music we may express such experiences as:

{ Happiness
{ Sadness

{ Love
{ Anger

{ Humor
{ Seriousness

{ Repose
{ Excitement

{ Motion
{ Rest

Each piece in this book is approached in two ways:

First, by explaining what it expresses; second, by showing, clearly and easily, how to realize that expression.

More advanced keys are introduced as the book progresses; the circle of fifths and the basis of key relationship are introduced.

This leads to a presentation of all major and minor scales. The student is introduced to the primary triads and their use in the formation of cadences. This is followed by arpeggios on the dominant seventh chord and the diminished seventh chord, as well as on the tonic chord of each key.

Modulation is explained in a simple manner and is adapted to the progression of scales through the circle of fifths. The major and minor scales, beginning on page 53, should be introduced when the student reaches the primary triads on page 30. From this point on, scale study and scale practice should be assigned in conjunction with the progressive lesson material presented in the book.

Howard Kasschau

EXPRESSION AND PERFORMANCE

Learning how to play the right notes is only the first step toward making music. To make music *speak,* to make it enjoyable to the performer and to the listener, the proper expression must be given each musical phrase. Only then can one achieve a satisfying musical performance.

Truly expressive piano playing is the result of the pianist's awareness of two important elements:

1. The means used by the composer to express a given emotion. This is conveyed by the character of the music, aided by the use of expression signs.

2. Careful attention by the performer to the full realization of the requirements expressed on the printed page.

Frequently Italian words are used to indicate various kinds of expression. Many of them are similar to their English translations. For instance:

agitato — agitated	*impetuoso* — impetuous
animato — animated	*maestoso* — majestic
deciso — decided	*marziale* — march-like
doloroso — doleful	*misterioso* — mysterious
energico — energetic	*passionato* — passionate
espressivo — expressive	*spiritoso* — spirited
grandioso — grand	*vivace* — vivacious

Good Morning, which appears on page 45 of Book One, is reprinted here. It is followed by three strongly contrasting versions which show how a composer may express different emotions. *It is important that the pianist develop the ability to listen carefully to his performance to insure the full expression of varying emotions.*

Good Morning

American Singing Game

1. A *happy* mood is suggested by the location of both hands in a higher register of the keyboard *(the treble clef).* The *vivace* and *forte* markings indicate brightness.

Vivace

44584c

2. A *sad* mood is suggested by the key of g minor. The repeated note in the bass is drum-like and threatening.

3. A *playful* mood is suggested by the spirited eigth-note figure as it alternates from left hand to right hand.

Good Morning and its three contrasting versions may be played as one composition.

Expression:

The *Allegretto* from the *Seventh Symphony* is a quiet piece, calm and full of repose. The lovely chord progressions must sound smooth and effortless. Each chord should not be loud but have a full sound. The general character of the piece is hymn-like.

Performance:

Play all the tones of each chord with equal strength to produce a warm, rich, quiet sound. A gentle downward motion of the wrists as each chord is played, and a gentle upward motion of the wrists as each chord is released will help to develop a flowing smoothness.

Allegretto

from the *Seventh Symphony*

Allegretto

Ludwig van Beethoven

A tempo indicates a return to the original tempo.

+4584

Expression:

Did You Ever See a Lassie is lively and humorous. The humor is expressed by the energetic accents at several places. The piece should be played at a lively tempo and without a *ritard.* at the end.

Performance:

Special attention should be paid to the accent sign, ($>$), placed over or under a note. This means that the accented note should be played with a *sudden loud tone.* An accented tone is produced by placing the finger over the key, then quickly and firmly pressing the finger to the bed (or bottom) of the key. Be careful to lighten the pressure on the next tone so that the sudden loudness occurs only on the tone that is marked by the accent.

Did You Ever See a Lassie?

American Singing Game Song

Expression:

Turn About Is Fair Play is a fast energetic piece. The scale passages are played by lifting the fingers high to produce a brilliant tone. The runs in both hands must fit together smoothly.

Performance:

This piece introduces sixteenth-notes, (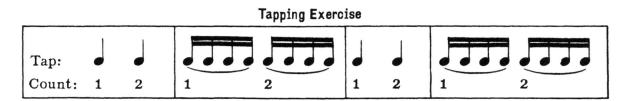). Four sixteenth-notes are played in one count. The following tapping exercise will help you hear the four sixteenth-notes in each count.

Turn About Is Fair Play

Expression:

The *Toreador Song* from the opera *Carmen* expresses excitement. *Carmen* is a story of Spanish gypsy life, love, dueling, bullfighting and many other adventures. This piece should sound bold and energetic. Strong rhythm and a firm tone will help create an exciting musical experience.

Performance:

The *Toreador Song* introduces a new rhythm, consisting of a dotted eighth-note and a sixteenth-note (). Since there are four sixteenth-notes in each quarter-note, the dotted eighth-note is equal to the first three of those sixteenth-notes, the fourth sixteenth-note being the one that is printed. The following tapping exercise will familiarize you with this rhythm.

An easy way to hear this rhythm when you are sight reading a piece is to hold the dotted eighth-note, then playing the following sixteenth-note only when you are ready to connect it quickly to the next note.

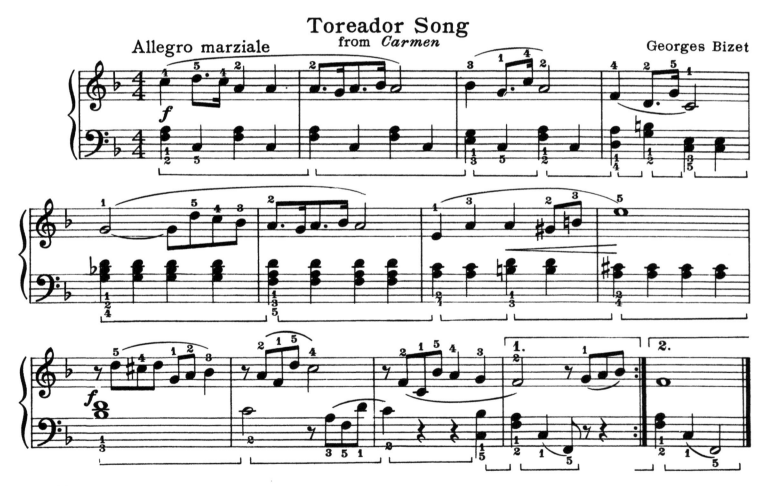

Bizet, one of the most distinguished French composers, is best known for his opera *Carmen*. All his life he lived in or near Paris. Although he was a remarkably fine pianist he was interested only in opera and compositions for orchestra, introducing many new and daring effects in his orchestrations. The *Toreador Song* is sung in the second act of the opera and has become a favorite of music lovers everywhere.

LEGER LINES AND SPACES

LEGER LINES are short lines added above or below the staff for notes that are not contained within the staff. LEGER SPACES are spaces that are bounded on one side or both sides by leger lines.

The leger lines and spaces below the G clef are actually a continuation of the lines and spaces of an imaginary F clef:

The leger lines and spaces above the F clef are actually a continuation of the lines and spaces of an imaginary G clef:

The leger lines above the G clef duplicate the F clef spaces three octaves *higher:*

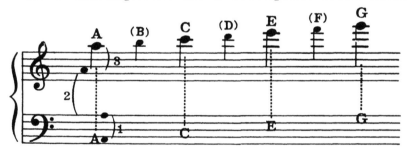

The leger lines below the F clef duplicate the G clef spaces three octaves *lower:*

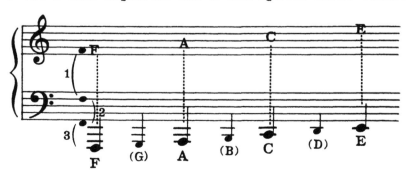

Expression:

Soldiers' March is one of the forty-three pieces contained in Schumann's *Album for the Young*. It is an energetic composition, and should be played quite fast. The rhythms must be very strict and very march-like. Play the tones of each chord *exactly* together to make each chord sound sharp and clear. The staccato must be really short to express liveliness.

Performance:

To produce an effective staccato, place the finger tips on the keys of the chord to be played, quickly throwing the hands into the key bed, at the same time raising the wrists and letting the wrists draw the hands into the air above the keyboard. This action is called the *rebound* — the hands rebound from the keyboard.

However, where the notes are marked with slurs, be sure to return to the basic keyboard touch, *legato.*

Soldiers' March
from *Album for the Young*

Allegro deciso

Robert Schumann

(1810-1856)

Robert Schumann began to study music when he was six years old. It was not long before he started to compose little pieces describing the people he met.

Many of Schumann's shorter compositions were musical descriptions of events and scenes he remembered of his childhood — the people he met, the places he visited. Among them are *Scenes from Childhood*, *Album for the Young* and *3 Sonatas for the Young* (dedicated to his three daughters). These and similar works were so important to Schumann that he thought the music he had written for children would live the longest. Most of his difficult pieces were written for and first performed by his wife, the pianist Clara Wieck.

Schumann was one of the great Romantic artists of the 19th century. In both his music and his writings (he was also very gifted in this field) he expressed the fanciful and emotional spirit of his times. Romantic music was often suggested by literary works and ideas, and some of Schumann's most famous works are no exception. For example: *Carnival, Papillons (Butterflies), Fantasy Pieces* and *Forest Scenes.*

Expression:

Moonlight expresses the repose of a calm restful evening that follows the close of a day. The piece is quietly flowing throughout and is played with subdued tones, in an unhurried tempo.

Performance:

The left hand, containing the melody, is played with a singing tone. The chords in the right hand should be played with a gentle downward motion and released with a gentle upward motion. The "loose wrist touch" was used in the *Allegretto* from Beethoven's *Seventh Symphony*, page 4.

Moonlight

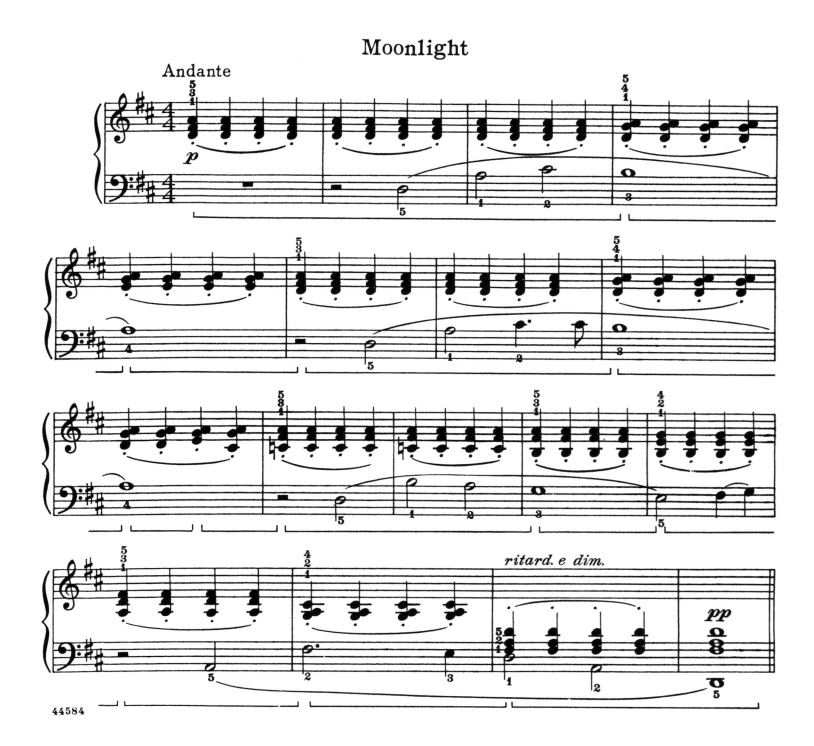

Expression:

Country Gardens is an old English folk tune. It was used as an accompaniment for a Handkerchief Dance by a group of traveling minstrels known as Morris Men. They journeyed from town to town giving performances, and were dependent upon the generosity of the various villagers for their livelihood. *Country Gardens* should be played in a lilting dance-like manner.

Performance:

A careful treatment of accents is essential to a good performance of this piece. The accents are on the first and third beats only; the second and fourth beats are played very lightly.

Country Gardens

English Handkerchief Dance

This famous composition of Franz Schubert, the first of three Military Marches, Op. 51, was written as a piano duet during the summer of 1822. Schubert's melodic source seemed to be endless, and this melody, like many others by him, is so natural and spontaneous that it has become one of the most universally popular pieces.

Marche Militaire

Franz Schubert, Op. 51 No.1

Allegro deciso

44584

The Battle Hymn of the Republic has an interesting history. During a visit to Washington, in 1861, Julia Ward Howe was captivated by the stirring qualities of the marching song, *John Brown,* then popular with the Union troops. She decided to set new words to it. The melody probably originated in South Carolina, and is known to have also been sung by Confederate soldiers to a variety of texts.

Expression and Performance:

The Battle Hymn of the Republic is a marching song and its rhythm is of utmost importance. The character of the melody is angular and the rhythm consists of a repeated dotted eighth- and sixteenth-note figure, (♩. ♪). Supporting the melody is a strong harmonic background which the left hand plays with a full resonant tone. The pedal must be maintained throughout each measure to supply the maximum amount of resonance.

The Battle Hymn of the Republic

Julia Ward Howe

Attributed to William Steffe

44384

For the further development of a *maestoso* style use "Solemn Procession" from the collection *Seven Recital Pieces* by Howard Kasschau. It is a stately recital piece in the key of c minor, and in 4/4 time.

44584

(1843-1907)

The life of Edvard Grieg centered around Bergen, Norway, where he lived and died. As a young man he studied in Germany and Denmark, but it was upon his return to Norway that he embarked upon his career as a composer. He is recognized as the one composer responsible for the development of a musical style that is completely expressive of the strong nationalistic feelings of the Norwegian people. He so thoroughly absorbed his country's folk-song heritage that his original melodies are hardly distinguishable from those of the folk-song literature.

Among his most popular compositions are the orchestral suites written for Henrik Ibsen's play, *Peer Gynt.* These were first published as piano duets. The character of Peer Gynt came to Ibsen after reading a folk tale found in the collection *Reindeer Hunting in the Rondë Hills.* Peer is one of the half-mythical, fantastic heroes of the Norwegian people. However, he had actually lived in Gudbranscal around 1800, and was an imaginative, genial, philosophical rascal.

Morning, the opening movement of the first *Peer Gynt Suite,* is quiet and contemplative.

Morning
from *Peer Gynt Suite I*

Edvard Grieg

44584

Expression and Performance:

The Glade in the Wood expresses a quiet gentle mood. The three counts in each measure should flow smoothly together and create the feeling of one basic pulse in each measure. The right hand should move over the left hand from one register to another in a relaxed manner.

The left hand is based upon two chords of the scale of A major. Here is a preparatory study for the left hand:

The Glade in the Wood

Waterfall is a study in repose. The quiet flowing melody in the left hand is played with a clinging pressure touch. This will produce a singing tone. The right hand plays a quietly moving accompaniment and must not overpower the left hand.

The climax in measures 17 through 24 should be large in thought and mood, not merely loud. This may be accomplished by a slight broadening of the tempo in these measures.

Waterfall

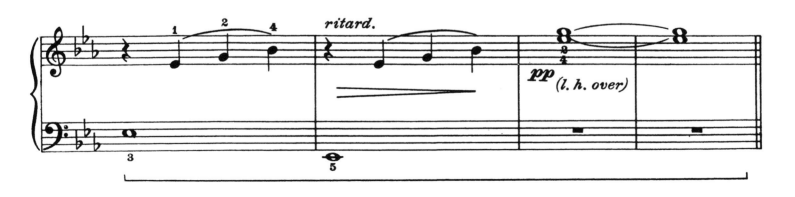

44584

VARIATION FORM

A *variation* is a transformation of a theme which, however, remains recognizable throughout. This transformation may be melodic, rhythmic or harmonic. All these devices are used in the variations upon *Pop! Goes the Weasel*. This piece is composed as follows:

Theme	{ The theme is in $\frac{6}{8}$ rhythm, marked *Allegro*. The melody, written in F major, is in the right hand. The harmonies are played by the left hand. }
Variation I	{ The theme is in $\frac{3}{4}$ rhythm, marked *Lento*. The melody, written in F minor, is played by the left hand. The harmonies are played by the right hand. }
Variation II	{ The theme is in $\frac{2}{4}$ rhythm, marked *Moderato*. The melody is again in F major and played by the right hand. The left hand plays an Alberti bass. }

Variations on
Pop! Goes the Weasel

Variation II
Moderato

Expression:

American Patrol is a typical military march. Strict rhythm must be maintained throughout with no *ritard.* at any point. The piece is uniformly loud with the exception of measures 17 to 24 which are played a bit more softly.

Performance:

A new time signature ($\frac{2}{2}$) is introduced in this piece. The time values are as follows:

= A half-note receives one count.

= Two quarter-notes are played in one count.

= Four eighth-notes are played in one count.

American Patrol

Allegro marziale

F. W. Meacham

SYNCOPATION

There are many forms of syncopation. It often occurs when a weak beat of a measure is tied over to a succeeding strong beat:

Syncopation also occurs when the weak portion of a beat is tied over to the following beat:

The charm of a syncopated rhythm lies in the *element of surprise;* the music seems to be momentarily suspended by an unexpected catching-up of the rhythm.

The following preparatory study should be learned *exactly*, with careful attention to the syncopation that occurs on the second beat.

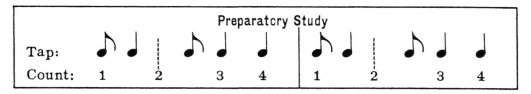

Fiesta

Allegro moderato

THE PRIMARY TRIADS

The PRIMARY TRIADS are the triads that are built upon the FIRST, FOURTH and FIFTH DEGREES of any major or minor scale. They are called the Tonic Triad (the first degree of the scale), Subdominant Triad (the fourth degree) and the Dominant Triad (the fifth degree).

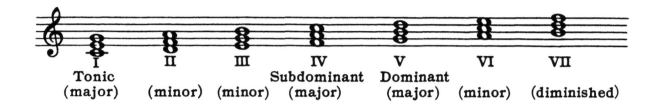

The primary triads are also called Cadence Chords. A CADENCE is an ending. Cadence Chords are used at the end of a phrase, a section, or an entire composition.

The Dominant Seventh Chord

The dominant triad may be enriched and made more active by the addition of a tone a SEVENTH ABOVE THE ROOT. This four-toned chord is called a Dominant Seventh Chord:

 The interval, from the root G to the top tone F, is a seventh.

The Dominant Seventh chord contains four tones and may appear in four positions:

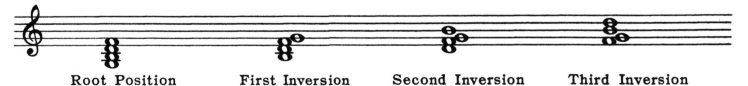

Root Position   First Inversion   Second Inversion   Third Inversion

The Major and Minor Scales, beginning on page 53, may be introduced at this point.

Expression:

Hungarisch portrays a feeling of patriotic enthusiasm. It suggests full-throated singing and lively dancing. A strong marching rhythm is also felt in the melody. The accents will increase the feeling of energy.

Performance:

Both hands should produce a full loud tone. The left hand carries the melody and should be played with a singing tone. Let the weight of the hand and arm press on the bed of each key *and* shift the weight from one finger tip to the next as the melody tones progress.

The chords should sound strong and rich. Be sure to apply an equal amount of pressure to all chord tones to produce this effect.

Hungarisch

Hungarian Folk Song

"Sahara Caravan" from the collection *Seven Recital Pieces* by Howard Kasschau is a performance piece and may be introduced at this time. The steady rhythm of the bass suggests the tread of camels. The chromatic line of the right hand chords affords an exotic quality associated with distant lands.

A-B: THE TWO-PART SONG FORM
(Binary Form)

A composition is written in *A-B form* (two-part song form or binary form) when it contains two contrasting parts, called Part A and Part B. Although the two parts are of different character they are musically related to each other in a way that creates a unified composition. In the following Swedish folk song Part A and Part B are both eight measures long; and the rhythm, ♩ ♫ ♩ is common to both parts. Notice the similarity of the last two measures of Part A and Part B.

Ox Dance

Minuet
from *Don Giovanni*

Wolfgang Amadeus Mozart

A *minuet* is a dance of French origin. The name is derived from the old French word *menu* meaning small, and refers to the short steps which are used in this dance. Originally, the minuet was a very short composition consisting of two eight-measure periods, each of which was repeated. A second minuet was soon added, usually written in three parts called a *trio*. The minuet in its lengthier form became a favorite dance at the courts of many countries during the eighteenth century.

44584

A-B-A: THE THREE-PART SONG FORM
(Ternary Form)

A composition is written in the *A-B-A form* (three-part song form or ternary form) when it contains three parts, the third part supplying an essential element of music, the element of *return*. In a three-part song form the first part, A, states a complete musical idea. The second part, B, is also a complete musical idea but of a new, contrasting character, *contrast* being another important element of music. The third part, A, *returns* to the musical material contained in the first part.

Minuet

Joseph Haydn

* A stress sign (—) indicates that more pressure is to be applied to a tone to lend a subtle emphasis.

44584

THE CODA

A *coda* is a passage which has been added to the ending of a composition. It is like an afterthought, as if the composer were reluctant to leave his composition. It varies in length, depending on the music. Some pieces have a coda of a few bars; others have a coda that becomes a new section in itself.

Wrong-Note Polka is written in a three-part song form with a coda.

Wrong-Note Polka

Part A (eight measures)

Coda (four measures)

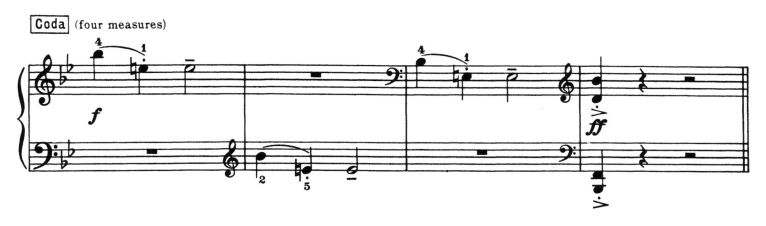

44584

THE ARPEGGIO IN EXTENDED FORM

When the notes of a chord are played one after the other, they form a broken chord which is called an *arpeggio*. This results in a sound like that produced by a harp. (The word *arpeggio* comes from the Italian *arpa,* meaning harp.)

An *arpeggio* is a frequently used musical device and considerable attention must be paid to the development of a competent arpeggio technic.

The thumb must pass under the other fingers in a relaxed manner, free of tension. The thumb must also remain relaxed when another finger is crossing over it. The arm should glide smoothly from one position to another without any sudden motion which would produce an uncontrolled accent.

Play the following preparatory studies many times, starting slowly and gradually increasing the speed. At first, practice hands separately; then practice hands together.

THE DOMINANT SEVENTH CHORD IN ARPEGGIO FORM
Preparatory Studies

40

The scales that have been studied so far are called *diatonic scales*. Diatonic scales are scales composed of five whole steps and two half-steps. The half-steps always occur between steps 3 and 4, and between steps 7 and 8. For example, in the scale of C major the notes E-F and B-C are the half-steps; all others are whole steps.

The *chromatic scale* consists of a succession of half-steps only, and therefore, involves the use of tones that are *foreign* to a given key.

It is important to play all the tones of the chromatic scale evenly. The thumb is used five times in each octave and must always produce *exactly* the same kind of tone as the other fingers, neither lighter nor heavier. The thumb must pass under the finger in a relaxed manner and should not be accompanied by a simultaneous movement of the forearm. Play the following preparatory studies with a gliding motion of the hand and forearm, concentrating upon loose fingers and a relaxed thumb.

First Preparatory Study
At first practice each hand separately; then practice hands together.

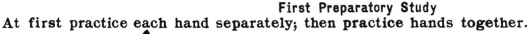

Second Preparatory Study
At first practice each hand separately; then practice hands together.

The Right Hand Chromatic Scale

The Left Hand Chromatic Scale

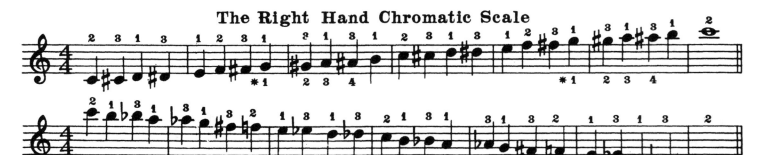

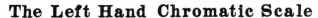

*This fingering permits greater speed. It is more difficult and should be introduced after the basic chromatic scale fingering has been learned.

Mad as a Hornet
Chromatic Scale Study

Johann Strauss, the younger, called the "Waltz King," was a world famous composer of dance music. He symbolized the gaiety of Viennese life. It was the wish of his father, also a famous composer of dance music, that none of his sons should become a musician. But the talent of Johann was so great that after a short career in banking, he turned to music and equalled the success of his illustrious father. After his father's death he organized several orchestras and toured Europe with them. To satisfy the demands of his enthusiastic audiences, he composed more than 500 waltzes, of which *Tales From the Vienna Woods* is one of the loveliest.

Tales from the Vienna Woods

Johann Strauss

Tempo di Valse (Introduction)

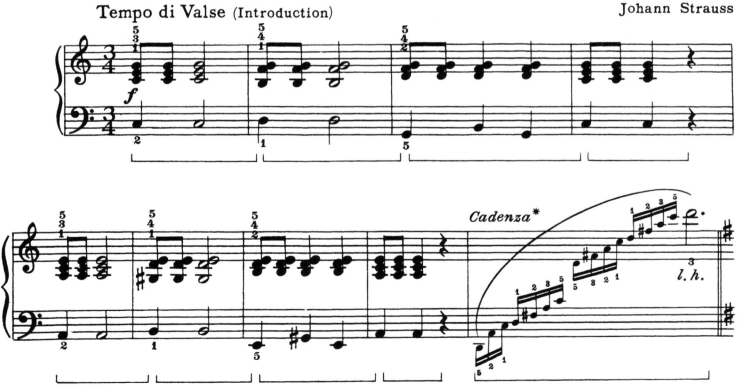

*A *cadenza* is a brilliant passage at the end of a section or movement. The rhythm is *completely free* and may be played as the performer chooses. Small notes are used to indicate this rhythmic freedom.

44584

"Call to the Hunt" from the collection *Seven Recital Pieces* by Howard Kasschau affords a brilliant and interesting performance piece. It may be introduced at this level.

THE DIMINISHED SEVENTH CHORD

A DIMINISHED SEVENTH CHORD is made up entirely of minor thirds. It may be spelled in a variety of ways, depending on the key in which it appears and its use within that key. For technical reasons, however, three Diminished Seventh Chords contain the *pianistic* problems of all other Diminished Seventh Chords.

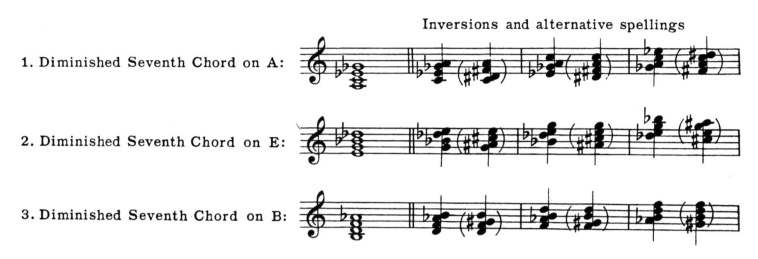

1. Diminished Seventh Chord on A:

2. Diminished Seventh Chord on E:

3. Diminished Seventh Chord on B:

THE DIMINISHED SEVENTH CHORD IN ARPEGGIO FORM
Preparatory Studies

The Diminished Seventh Arpeggio on A

*This fingering is more difficult but has the advantage of placing the longer fingers on the black keys.

Preparatory Studies

The Diminished Seventh Chord on E

Preparatory Studies

The Diminished Seventh Arpeggio on B

44584

THE TRILL

The TRILL is an ornamental figure requiring the rapid and even playing of two notes, only one of which is written on the page. These two notes may be a half-step or a whole step apart. The lower note is called the PRINCIPAL NOTE and is the note written on the page. The upper note, not written on the page, is the next scale-step above the written note (either a half-step or a whole step) and is called the AUXILIARY NOTE.

This is the sign for the trill:

Preparatory Trill Studies
Right Hand Alone

Left Hand Alone

Soaring

(1824-1884)

Smetana was a native of Bohemia. His father was an amateur musician. Like Mozart, Smetana was a youthful prodigy. He was an accomplished pianist at the age of six, and when he was eight he composed dance tunes. While a young man he studied piano and composition in Prague. During this time he gathered impressions of the Czech people and the Czech countryside that influenced his later writings in operatic and symphonic forms.

In 1848 Bohemia was torn by revolution. By the time peace was restored, eleven years later, a strong feeling of nationalism had developed in the hearts of the people. They demanded a theatre for plays and operas given in the Czech language. Here was the true value of Smetana's art. His creative genius provided a powerful stimulus to the rebirth of the national spirit of his countrymen.

The symphonic poem, from which this melody is taken, describes the beauty of the Moldau, a river which flows across Bohemia and joins the Elbe.

Theme
from *The Moldau*

Bedřich Smetana

* *sfz (sforzando)* is a marking used to indicate the playing of a tone or chord with sudden, explosive emphasis.

44584

IDENTIFICATION OF KEYS, USING THE KEY SIGNATURES

When there are sharps in the key signature the first note of the key (the tonic) is a half-step above the last sharp.

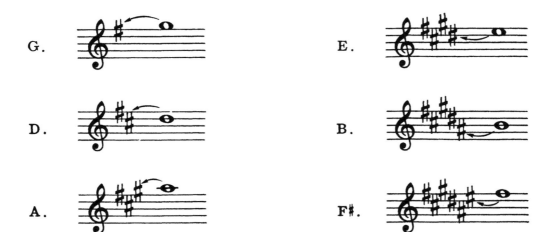

When there are flats in the key signature the next-to-last flat *is* the first note of the key (the tonic).

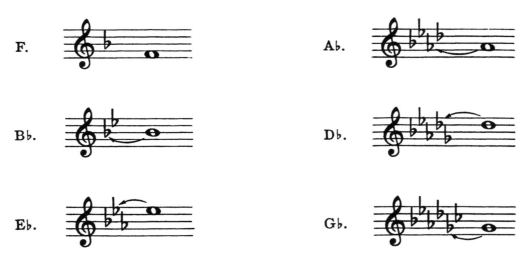

MODULATION

Modulation is the process of going from one key to another. There are three types of modulation:

1. *Diatonic* — going from one key to a key related to it. (For instance, from C major to G major)

2. *Chromatic* — going from one key to a key not related to it. (For instance, from C major to A-flat major)

3. *Enharmonic* — going from one key to another when the pitch remains the same, but the *spelling* of the notes changes. (For instance, from F-sharp major to G-flat major)

Diatonic modulation is presented here as the scales progress through related keys.

The Play of Fountain Waters

Moderato e teneramente

mp (second time pp)

l. h.

C major

I

The F♯ introduces a modulation.

poco ritard.

Cadence in G

V7

I.

"Gumbo Lumbo" from the collection *Seven Recital Pieces* by Howard Kasschau is a graceful study in velocity and interlaced passage playing. It makes an excellent performance piece and may be introduced at this time.

44584c

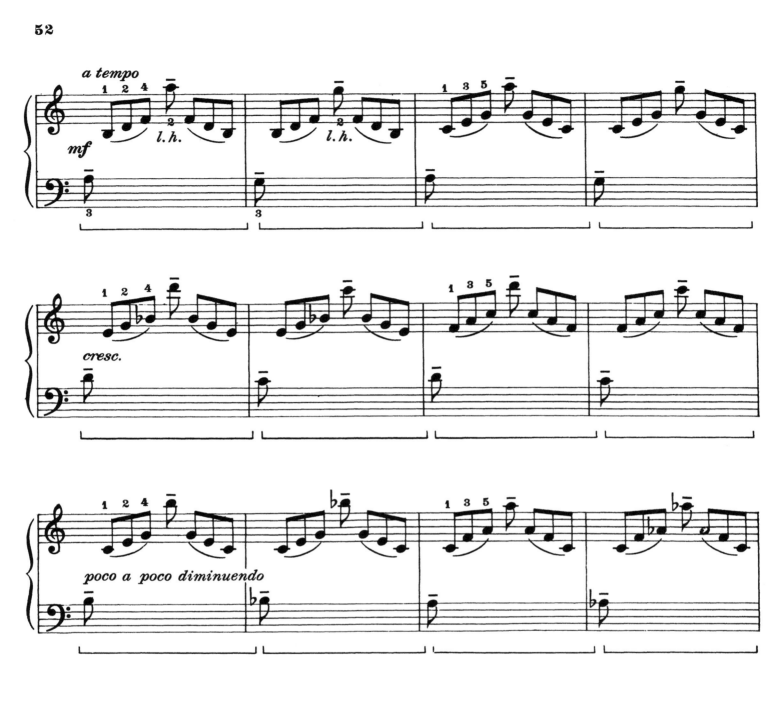

Cadence in C
V7   I

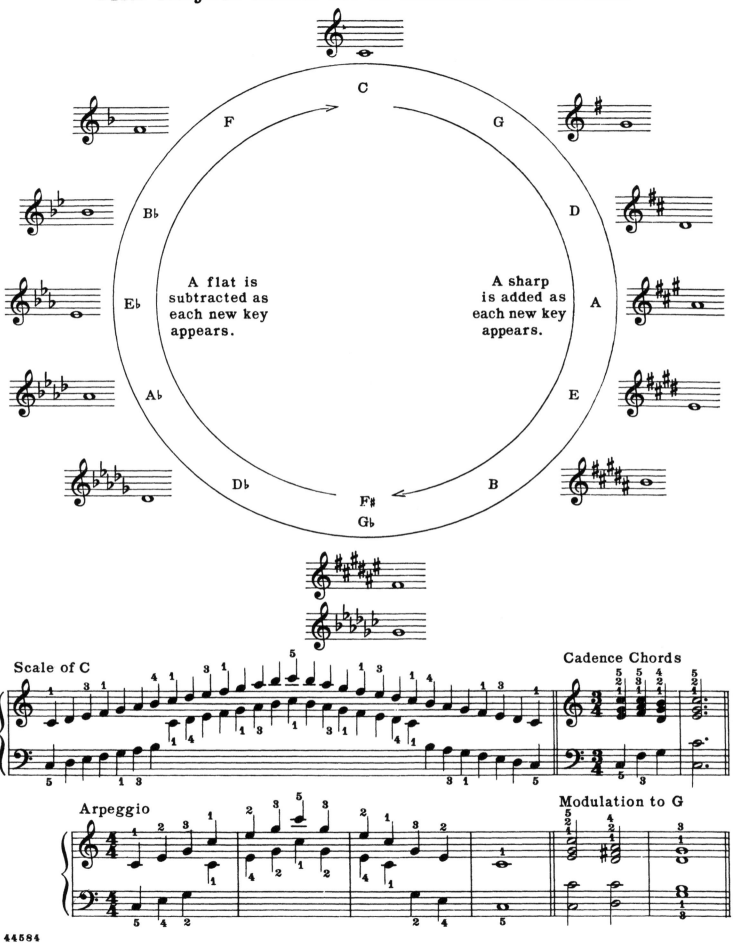

Scale of E

Arpeggio

Cadence Chords

Modulation to B

Scale of B

Arpeggio

Cadence Chords

Modulation to F♯

Scale of F♯

Arpeggio

Cadence Chords

The keys of F♯ (six sharps) and G♭ (six flats) use the same keys with different spelling.

44584

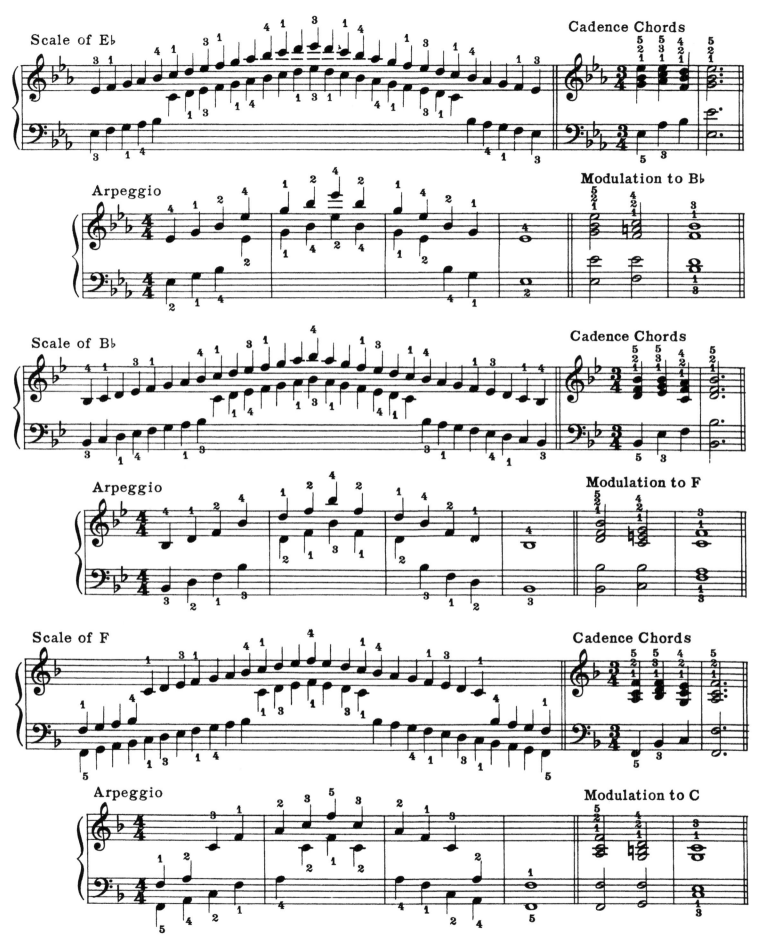

THE MINOR KEYS
The Relative Minor Approach

Every major scale has a Relative minor scale. The Relative minor scale begins on the sixth note of any major scale.

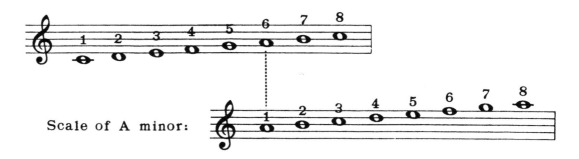

Scale of C major:

Scale of A minor:

Any minor scale may appear in three different forms:

The Natural Minor
This is the original form of the minor scale. The natural minor scale begins and ends on the sixth note of its relative major scale. For example, A minor begins and ends on the sixth note, A, of the scale of C major.

Ascending   Descending

The Harmonic Minor
This is the most frequently used form of the minor scale. The seventh note is raised a half-step to provide a more active leading tone.

#7   #7

The Melodic Minor
This is a more recent form of the minor scale. The lack of a skip, as in the Harmonic minor scale, allows a smoother melodic line. The sixth and seventh notes are sharped ascending and natural descending.

#6 #7   ♮7 ♮6

MINOR SCALES

A minor (relative to C major)

E minor (relative to G major)

B minor (relative to D major)

F# minor (relative to A major)

C# minor (relative to E major)

G# minor (relative to B major)

44584

CERTIFICATE AWARD

This Award certifies that

....

has successfully completed

BOOK TWO

and is now ready to advance to

BOOK THREE

of

THE *Howard Kasschau Piano Course*

_____
Teacher

Date_____